Stories of changing lives

The Patients' Council, Royal Edinburgh Hospital

Stories of changing lives

Artist: James

Stories of changing lives

'We delight in the beauty of the butterfly, but rarely admit the changes it has gone through to achieve that beauty.'

Maya Angelou

A Patients' Council (Royal Edinburgh Hospital) publication
ISBN: 978-0-9564438-09
Butterfly images created by members and staff of Functionsuite, an Artlink project based in the Royal Edinburgh Hospital.

Acknowledgements

The Patients' Council would like to thank everyone involved for their support in making 'Stories of Changing Lives' a reality. Special thanks go to all our contributors for sharing their experiences and thinking which gave life to this publication.

Lesley Smith for taking the lead and her sensitive work in producing this publication.

To our own members and staff, past and present, in particular David Budd, Elaine Dobbie, Albert Nicolson, Bruce McNally, Maggie McIvor, Alison Robertson, Ruth Rooney, Patricia Whalley.

Julia Fitzpatrick (Inspiring Inclusion) for mentoring and supporting Lesley.

Our additional steering group members Ivan Barry (Circles Network), Cathy Carpenter (CRT), Dr. Fiona Clunie, Susan McMeel (CRT) Jo McFarlane, Alison Roy (Carr-Gomm Scotland), Susan Tennyson (REH), Andy Wills (REH) also Murray Chalmers (Chaplain). Andy Egerton (Places for People).

Jeanette Bell, James McIntyre, Stewart Murray, Phyllis Swan and Anne Elliot – members and staff of Functionsuite, an Artlink project based in the Royal Edinburgh Hospital – for the artwork throughout and helping to plan the cover design.

To The Graphics Company (www.graphics.coop) for taking our ideas and designing a publication that exceeded our expectations.

NHS Lothian Endowments for funding this publication.

Stories of changing lives

Artist: Jeanette

Contents

Introduction Lesley Smith	1
A butterfly's lesson	6
Dreams do come true Moe	8
Queens Bab's got her royal bed! Michelle	14
Coming full circle Richard	22
I did it my way! Joan	32
Recovering in the community James	38
My home is where my heart is Norman	44
Getting my life back! Mary	48
Reflections	58
Creating a desirable future Susan McMeel	60
Reflections – Person Centred Planning Julie	63
Let people who… Jennifer Simpson	64
Morningside and beyond Terry O'Malley	66
It's cool! Pete	68
Taking the first step Alison Roy	76
Recovery, reprovisioning, helicopter or tunnel – whatever it takes! Carl Abernethy	78
And finally…! Alison Robertson and Lesley Smith	82
Glossary	86

Contributors have chosen whether to use their own name or a pseudonym. All other names have been changed and services made anonymous to protect confidentiality.

Introduction

The Patients' Council is a collective advocacy organisation representing the views of the people who use the services of the Royal Edinburgh Hospital (Mental Health). We are a user-led, independent collective advocacy organisation where our very active members are represented on many working groups in the provision of the hospital's services. Our aim is to ensure that the voice of the service user is heard and that the services best meet the needs of the people for whom they are provided and speaking out when they are not; ensuring that support and care is of a high quality and recovery-focused.

A couple of years ago we were talking about the quality of support offered to people when they are discharged from the hospital and we found a wide variance from 'fantastic' to 'support – what's that?' As we talked more we realised that many of the good experiences appeared to be related to a team known as the Multi-Agency Team (MAT) and their way of working known as person-centred. Not everyone knew this team because they were focused on supporting people move out from the continuing care services of the hospital. We felt that not only did we want to know more but that their way of working should be available for everyone. As we learnt more, we realised that the MAT team worked with people at a time of re-provisioning (bed closures) in the hospital. We felt that this was an important piece of work in terms of service provision and also in terms of the profound effect on people's lives which we wanted to record and share with a wider audience.

We arranged a meeting and asked hospital-based staff and social care providers who were all involved to a meeting to share our idea and see if there was any interest. Overwhelmingly there was and after securing funding through NHS Endowments we formed a steering group with a diverse membership of ourselves, interested NHS staff and support providers to begin planning. I was tasked with interviewing people and bringing the project together. 'Stories of Changing Lives' is what we have achieved.

'Stories of Changing Lives' is about giving a voice for people to share their personal experiences with the focus being on moving on to community-based care. This happened in the mid/late 1990's when policy changed and the recognition that hospital-based care was no longer a viable option for people who have been assessed as having a long term mental illness. The Royal Edinburgh Hospital set about re-provisioning their continuing care wards and hostels.

In all, over 100 people were discharged into the community with a variety of living options made available in partnership with support providers and housing associations. For some people this meant their own flat, for others it meant sharing in a variety of living arrangements. All support was personalised and tailored to each individual's strengths and needs. A new team was created called the Multi-Agency team (MAT), who acted as co-ordinators for the whole process and became care managers for each person. As the re-provisioning process was completed, funding was changed and the MAT team gave way to a new team, the Community Rehabilitation Team (CRT), with many of the same people, who carried on the care manager role. There was also a Mental Health Partnership overseeing the whole process.

For many people with a diagnosis of mental illness it is all too easy for their experiences to be reduced to case notes or a diagnosis. An official report or evaluation of the re-provisioning process would miss the real experience of the impact for the people whose lives have changed. This publication seeks to turn this on its head and give a space for people's reality in their own words and with their personal experiences to be expressed and acknowledged. Whilst this publication includes the word 'Stories' in its title the experiences are in no way fiction as perhaps the word may imply.

How we would ask people if they would like to be involved was a challenge. We, at the Patients' Council, knew there were over 100 people who moved out of hospital but we didn't know who they were. We produced an information pack about the project, our aims and contact details and the Community Rehabilitation Team (CRT), in their role as Care Managers, agreed to contact people on our behalf. As people expressed an interest I would meet with them to discuss the project in more depth and for them to decide if it was something they would like to be part of. We would meet again, in a place that they felt comfortable, usually their home, and I would record an interview, with written agreement, that would be transcribed and drafted into their contribution. We would meet again to discuss the draft and make any changes or corrections and agree a final copy. Everyone had the option to change their mind at any point and withdraw until they signed off the final copy for publication. Everyone was involved throughout and I met with people as often as was needed or asked for.

In all, seven people share their experiences as a record but more importantly as an insight, inspiration and hope for others and, if we are being honest, a challenge. We decided it would be good to balance the book with reflections from some of the people who, as professionals, supported people as not only their living circumstances changed but also their lives. Some professionals agreed to a reflection whilst others offered us more detailed insights which we, at the Patients' Council, are deeply grateful for. By being open themselves they have entered into the spirit of this book and truly help the reader gain a fuller understanding and rounded picture. Some people would say that community care doesn't work but we ask you to think again: these stories prove that when community-based care is focused, well planned and resourced in a person-centred and holistic way it enables people to be in control of their lives showing that it can and does work.

Whilst reading people's experiences you can get a sense of what it was that individually they found helpful. In reading the professionals' contributions you can understand the principles, values and enthusiasm of how they worked to support people, their family members when they were involved, and working in partnership with other professionals. Bringing the varied contributions together highlights how when individuals and professionals work together, where the person is central and in the driving seat, positive change happens.

Initially many were sceptical whether the re-provisioning was the way forward, questioning whether it was right and whether people would be able to cope with living outside of a hospital-based care environment. Read on and find out for yourself. I know that when I was meeting people, hearing their experiences and creating this book it has been hard not to try and comment on or evaluate aspects of mental health care but that was not the aim of 'Stories of Changing Lives'. The aim was to let people speak for themselves and by sharing their experiences contributors have offered us, as readers, an insight into their lives. Remember it takes courage to contribute as they can only anticipate how they would be received. Read on in the spirit of hope that people had when contributing – to share, to be heard and to encourage others that, 'if I can do it, anyone can!'

I learnt so much from hearing people's experiences and as someone who has also spent many years in and out of hospital, including a rehabilitation ward, and resided in a number of supported living services, I found myself relating with many of people's experiences and the challenges they faced. For me, once I was able to take control of aspects of my life I began to not only recover my life but thrive. I found myself admiring each person's strength whilst also picking up a few tips and insights along the way for myself. I feel truly honoured, humbled and inspired by the privilege of meeting all the people who contributed and to my work on this project.

We chose the metaphor of the butterfly as a theme for 'Stories of Changing Lives' as it aptly encapsulates the journey of change and growth that every contributor has taken.

Lesley Smith

'The past is a place of reflection, not a place of residence.'

A butterfly's lesson

One day, a small opening appeared in a cocoon. A man sat and watched for the butterfly for several hours as it struggled to force its body through that little hole.

Then it seemed to stop making any progress.

It appeared as if it had got as far as it could and it could not go any further.

So the man decided to help the butterfly. He took a pair of scissors and opened the cocoon. The butterfly then emerged easily.

But it had a withered body, it was tiny with shriveled wings.

The man continued to watch. He expected that at any moment the wings would open, enlarge, expand and become firm, enabling the butterfly's body to be supported.

None of this happened.

In fact the butterfly spent the rest of its life crawling around with a withered body and shriveled wings. It never was able to fly.

What the man in his kindness and his goodwill did not understand was that the restricting cocoon and the struggle required for the butterfly to get through the tiny opening were natures way of forcing fluid from the body of the butterfly into its wings. It would be ready for flight once it achieved its freedom from the cocoon.

It is the struggle that enables the butterfly to not only gain its freedom... but also to take its flight.

Sometimes struggles are exactly what we need in our lives.

If we were to go through our lives without any difficulties it would cripple us.

We would not be as strong as we could have been. We would never been able to fly!

Dreams do come true

By Moe

I've got my own business you know, it's great. Having a job, something to do, is very important and it totally changes your whole idea of life. I have money to buy music, clothes, budgies and cold water fish, all the things I like.

My business is car valeting. Initially my psychiatrist was very helpful getting me the job of washing hospital cars and being paid as I could earn so much without it affecting my benefits. I work just myself as the pay wouldn't be worth my while splitting it. I have also built up my own set of tools, including a power jet cleaner, and printed off business cards. I also do a bit of gardening so really I do a lot of things. It's great! I used to go to the Horticulture Project in the hospital which I loved. The worker was fair chuffed with me as I had gone every time I was to go and I was pleased with myself, 'we are doing good' I thought. It came time for me to move on though and I was quite disappointed at losing the horticulture. I had my car washing though and I had progressed onto a suitable wage so I could expand and I did.

Even though I was in and out of hospital for years after my first admission I had an easy enough time. The drugs were'nae working for us though and I was getting tremendous voices all because of feelings entering my body. I was in a really bad way until I got onto a new medication in the rehabilitation ward and it became a changing point in my life. I wasn't too happy at first as the medication was given by injection and I hated the needle but I've got used to it now. It's not always easy as I have my not so good days, some bad times as well but I know what helps me which is reassuring because sometimes it's quite difficult to put 'a top on it'.

When I was in the hospital I was lying in my bed all day because there was nothing for me to do. The only thing to look forward to was the tea trolley. It wasn't healthy, so I'm quite pleased that my consultant proposed the car washing to me and I thought, 'whoo, if I do a good job of this I will get the contract' and I did working for the NHS.

I also used to go to the sports centre to play badminton which I liked but I didn't have any friends to continue it with. I have made a few friends along the way but as we've all gone our own ways we only see each other in the passing. As I've said my psychiatrist was the life and soul of the change in my life really because of the job.

Anyway, it was 'time to leave the nest' as they say and move out of hospital. I wasn't too happy about it, the thought of being stuck in a house all the time. I mean you get used to things on the wards, the coming and going, the casual chat, the cigarettes, the tea and all the paraphernalia that goes along with it. You get used to it, quite fond of it actually and that's what I felt apprehensive about losing going back out to the community. I still had the job but that didn't make things easier and I was quite scared. I really didn't want to leave and I was scared of living outside the hospital again. At first, when I would go out with someone to do stuff the charge nurse would say, 'I want you to do this, I know you are able to do this, come on' and I thought 'right ok, kick up the arse and see what we can do,' so I did. When I was out and about I found it helpful to have people go with me so sharing buses with members of staff was very helpful, as I felt reassured. I started taking bus rides to places with people and starting cycling into Morningside to the shops, library *etc.*, just picking up bits and pieces.

I think the money I earned has been a gift as it has helped me regarding the other things that were not available to have. That in itself has encouraged me. One time when I was collecting my wages in the hospital I saw a notice that said 'get on your bike and do something about it' so I thought that was a great idea and I was able to buy myself a bike from my wages. I hear voices and sometimes the voices have said to me 'you are cycling, you are not well' and 'you are well, you are cycling'. I would talk back saying, 'no, it's got nothing to do with that' and just got on with whatever I was doing at the time. Now I go into town and on holidays with my bicycle and trailer. I have been to Peebles with one of my key workers, and I normally go down to a campsite outside Musselburgh, for three or four weekends during the holiday season camping. I use my bike to travel and the money I earn to buy food and music.

One of my favourite things is also going for teas. My favourite is warm croissants with jam, butter, and a pot of tea. There is a café near me which is really nice, especially if you get the sofa seats. What it actually does, is it sort of hits the topic. If something is good for you and you enjoy it then you need to maintain it which is why I got the bike. I think it's entirely up to the person themselves to change their life and the support is all geared to help you to recover from whatever your problems are at the time. My support has certainly given me the opportunity to do so – from the doctor, the nurses, horticulture and the support staff where I stay. I might never have asked my consultant about the job and if I hadn't I would still have been on a couple of pounds a week.

I moved to a hostel from the hospital, it was outreach I think. You had members of staff coming in the morning and you had to do your chores. I had to move out of there and I didn't want to but they said I had no option. I think it was more so that it was time for me to do so and they wanted me to better my standard of life. It was time to move on as they say.

I met staff from a new support organisation when I was at the hostel and about to move into a shared house. I was apprehensive meeting them and about what would take place, what they would think of me and all that as I'd been supported by other support organisations but they were smiling and I felt welcome. This is good I thought, 'I've passed!' This new home and support were another changing point in my life. The hospital had nominated this organisation as my support team and everything went well. I moved into the shared house and the staff recognised qualities in me and thought, 'oh, he seems to be doing fine on his own' as I was cooking, shopping and making meals. I was able to make my oatie biscuits and cakes which I loved baking. I was able to bake because I made enough money from my car washing to buy the ingredients. Sharing in the house though could be a bit frightening as I was scared of someone and I didn't know how to react.

As I said my support workers saw qualities that I was able to look after myself and one of them proposed a move to a different place where people looked after their own finances and they were given money for care though still a bit like the shared house. When I first saw the place I thought it was absolutely dingy, damp, like a hell! My support worker told me not to worry as they were going to paint it and put carpets down for me so I thought 'great, ok'. I wanted to do that myself though and I was uncertain about moving again but once I moved in, I put in my own touches and odds and ends. The first couple of weeks in this new place I focused on decorating. I stripped all the walls down and sanded the fireplace leaving stickers for what colour of paint to use as well. I can do lots of things – it's great!

In the house it's a give and take thing for us as sometimes I make meals for the others. I might deprive them for a couple of weeks of my cooking then I'll bring back the chicken dinners and they go 'great, brilliant'! I also studied cookery at college and I got on great with loads of people while there. I had a brilliant time learning what an experience cooking can be and got a certificate as well! When you have the rudiments of cooking, it's quite easy to put together. I love Chinese and Italian food especially Spaghetti Bolognese but nobody in the house does because it is too fiddly and can be messy. It's great because I put basil, tomatoes, garlic and a little sugar into the sauce. The rawness of the tomatoes is mellowed down by the sugar. I love trying new things, even got myself a bread maker to expand my repertoire.

I have more freedom now than being in hospital. I have a care manager from the Community Rehabilitation Team (CRT) and he pops in from time to time and helps with any problems I have. My benefits were held up once so he helped me phone up a couple of times as there is so much bureaucracy around them. I get all my benefits now and it really does help. I can go out whenever I want. I used to go to see Horse, I love her music, and my support worker could be a friend to go along with. The support workers remind me about my medication and making sure that everything is ticking over but I don't give it that much of a thought, really, as they are in tune with my needs and things. I pay for that care anyway, so I suppose if I say that I want to go to the theatre then we can go. I feel that if there is anything I need to do I can go to them and talk it through. It's a 24 hour service and it's costing me quite a packet though that's what my benefits are for. They are worth the money and I find them ok. If anything comes up they help me.

They are great laddies and lassies – they paid me to say that!

Dreams do come true 13

Artist: Phyllis

Queen Bab's got her Royal bed!

By Michelle

When my mum, Babs, was pregnant with me, there was a fire in her house and it was gutted. It's reckoned that mum was so traumatised by the fire and the death of her cat that it was the trigger for her schizophrenia. It really manifested itself after I was born as the scare of losing me, a much wanted baby, was very stressful for her. It just goes to show that it could happen to anyone, that if you are under too much stress you can just go into yourself.

Mum had been in hospital a number of times over the years but the last time was for almost 18 years and she was as institutionalised as anyone could be. Her life, at the time, revolved around the regime of the ward and the hospital. She had her routine and was always rushing off to somewhere and didn't want to miss out on anything. Dare anyone interfere with her routine as even I had to plan my visits around her! I used to visit around a mealtime because I knew I would get her full attention and if the evening was nice we would go for a walk around the hospital grounds. My mum loved fresh flowers and always had a vase that would need replenishing so that would become our task. She would be in her wheelchair and anything she spotted it was my mission to get some, even if it meant a bit of climbing over flowerbeds. Her job was to watch out for any security but we were never caught.

When mum first mentioned that she had been approached about moving out of the hospital I wasn't sure what she was meaning. As I heard more about people being moved into the community my first thought was 'they are so desperate to sell off the land, it's just a mass clear out to make millions'. I wondered where everyone would go and that this really was not any good. Many questions were going through my mind about what would happen if people became ill while at home? Where would home be? What if someone needed to go into the hospital, even for a short time, would there even be any beds? Then mum and I had a meeting with Elizabeth and Phillip from the MAT where I was able to learn more. They explained that mum would have her own flat with support workers as well as a MAT worker, Elizabeth, who would keep in frequent contact with mum and that the psychiatrist would visit mum at home. This sounded good as I couldn't imagine my mum being honest about anything that troubled her as she would be too scared that she would end up back in hospital. The fact that somebody would come to her and keep in close contact with her in her environment made a big difference. After having been in hospital for many years people didn't trust that they would be able to come home again 'aye, they said that years ago and I'm still here', I heard many people say when visiting mum. So knowing there would be a safety net was good and that people weren't being abandoned to 'tough, you're out now so just get on with it.'

The next part was deciding where mum would live. A Housing Association had just completed building new flats in an area mum said she would like to live and where she had grown up so she was offered one. It was like going back to her roots. There were 14 flats offered to people moving out of the hospital so all the support would be provided by one support organisation. Everyone would have their own flat and the support staff would also have a flat as a base and be there 24 hours a day so I was reassured that mum wasn't going to just be left.

As mum had many physical support needs as well she was allocated a specially adapted flat on the ground floor and she was really excited about the prospect of getting her own home and moving out of the hospital. It was so good to see her enthusiasm, though she said that all the organising could be left to me as she just wanted to be there as quickly as possible! I, on the other hand, had to quickly get to grips with planning. A care plan was developed based on how mum said she would like to spend her time and her needs. At first I queried the number of support hours for mum as I thought there wasn't enough and that there could be long periods where my mum could be left on her own. I didn't think this would be good for her mental health especially as she had been so used to being around people but also because of her physical related support needs. I did challenge the hours and we negotiated an agreement as I did with other plans where I considered there could be a potential risk for mum.

Mum was one of the first to be offered a flat but because of all the adaptations needed she ended up being the last person to actually move and this frustrated her. She was so keen to move it was good that the staff flat had a resource room for all the service users so mum would regularly go down and spend some time there, getting to know the others and ensuring that she was involved. Some people she knew from around the hospital but others she didn't and there was no way she wanted to miss out. In fact she was so keen that one day she went into Morningside, bought a turkey before hailing a cab and arriving at the staff flat announcing that she had brought the Christmas dinner!

As we planned, what was really good was that everything did come down to 'what was the right/best thing for Babs?' Mum liked to be able to do things for herself but considering her health many things could be risky but everyone worked with this and at times I did challenge the team as 'good enough wasn't good enough!' We became very creative and resourceful in ensuring mum could be as independent as possible. Mum didn't like getting up early and for that reason missed breakfast whilst in hospital because they had such a tight routine that if you weren't there it wasn't kept for you. Yet in her home the support staff responded to this by providing support at the times that she needed them so they would come around 10.30am to help her get washed and ready for the day. It could also mean that if no-one was around and she fell how long could she lie there? Or what if she decided to go off for a walk and no-one would know where she was? A number of ways round this were initially to provide mum with a personal alarm that she could wear around her neck that was linked to the staff base, and additionally movement sensors in her flat were fitted so that if she got out of bed the sensor would ring in the staff base. Having the sensor system meant that support staff could then be there and give her the support and help she needed in her own space and time. The same with leaving her flat, so this and many other things showed that we were all taking risk seriously. The person-centred planning and support was purely for mum and how to best to meet her needs. We had to think about what mum would be likely to do and anticipate any problems so that they could be addressed without mum losing her independence. The last thing we wanted was for mum to move from one institution to another.

When mum did move in she had everything that she wanted. There was a furnishings grant and she took great pride in shopping and choosing what she needed and wanted. A really big deal for her was to have a double bed that was all hers especially after spending years in a hard, single hospital bed-for her, this was luxury. She also wanted a sofa bed, which at first, some of the staff couldn't get their head around but mum insisted that she wanted somewhere for people to stay over if she wanted. I agreed and pointed out that it was normal to have guests stay over in your own home. If it was good enough for others then mum was no different after all no-one was getting to share her bed!

I did have to, at times, remind the care team that this was going to be someone's home for life not a mini hospital or institution so I would challenge the professionals' thinking at times but I always explained why I was saying what I was and I was always listened to. I worried a bit that I was seen as 'Michelle the pessimist' always having some point to raise but mum said that she wanted me to deal with the practical side of her move and it was my job to make sure that everything was in place for her and that she wouldn't be abandoned or left in a risky situation. What is good is we all became close through supporting mum and I still keep in contact with some. Mind you I didn't let on to Elizabeth at the time that I had a friend, who I had grown up with and knew mum, helping me think through all the practical adaptations for mum's flat and how they could be resourced or funded-they had studied Occupational Therapy together. We did laugh about it when I eventually confessed!

It was great to watch mum develop her own way of being because let's face it she was incredibly institutionalised. Mum found it a hard adjustment at first realising that she could choose what she could eat and planning her meals but she soon got the hang of it and her favourite would be steak which was something that wouldn't have been on the menu in the hospital! As she realised that tea didn't have to be at 5pm and that she could have a drink whenever she wanted one, this was liberating for her. Mum delighted in going and doing her own food shopping with her support worker and would plan to go later on a Friday afternoon so that she could then go for a fish tea. It was even better when she got her own car, through the motability scheme, as it gave her so much freedom to go where she wanted, when she wanted. If she fancied an ice-cream in Musselburgh and to sit by the harbour she could without worrying that she had to be back for a certain time. It would have been easy to just have done things for mum but that wouldn't have been right and seeing her making all her choices and showing them to me was great. Mum chose her car making sure that it would fit all her practical needs including carrying her wheelchair as well as in a colour she liked. The support organisation ensured that her support workers had a driving licence and relevant insurance.

Mum still kept herself busy but she chose how busy she would be and how she spent her time. When mum was in hospital she would refuse to go to Occupational Therapy as she wasn't impressed with what was on offer: 'Who do they think I am?' she would say 'all they ever do is make candles or stuff envelopes' so she loved to do want she wanted now, whether going to a pub quiz with her friends or to a show with me. I would go round for tea and we would just chill out with a film and have a good laugh. It was just about being normal and doing normal things together.

A big change for mum was actually getting money as she had no concept of how to manage so much money after being so long in hospital. For years she only had £13 a week for pocket money and had no need for a bank account. She also had no idea how much things like bread and milk cost because she never had to think about it, meals were just there as if by magic on the ward. So she had to learn and proved to be really good at keeping a budget and making sure she had money for bills, food, socialising and her cigarettes! It was good that she had that control and also the support to help her do so.

...scination was for the royal family so going
... to London with her support workers was
...ed it, including the travel as she had never
... was a bit cheeky though as when she was

discussing whether someone was wearing a wig or not on the plane she put her hand over and gave it a wee lift to prove a point! She loved that trip and would have gone on more if she hadn't become unwell-she was gutted that she wouldn't get on her planned trip to France. She had had some difficulties when in hospital with choking when she was eating and around the same time she also lost a lot of weight even though nothing else in her life had changed to explain this loss. It was only when she found it more difficult in her home that tests showed that mum had developed cancer of the oesophagus.

For people who are in a similar situation to me, caring for someone, if you aren't happy about something don't just sit back. Put your point across and if you feel that people aren't listening or dismissive just keep on being persistent. If you don't feel in your gut that something is right then speak up. After all if you want people to be as happy as they can be you have to put yourself in their position and ask 'would I like to live like that?' or 'how would I like my house to be?' and get others to ask the same question of themselves.

Ultimately stick with how you feel and do your best for the person as it's worth it. My mum got her life back and it was great to see the change in her with so many happy memories to treasure.

Queen Bab's got her Royal bed! 21

Artist: Phyllis

Coming full circle

By Richard

The way I see it I left growing up, going through adolescence, a bit late which explains how, even though I had a happy, carefree childhood, things became more complicated as I grew older and probably had something to do with how I first came into hospital. I felt puberty hit me like a train and I was frightened by this oncoming adulthood. All these feelings coming over me felt dramatic and I wanted my childhood to go on.

I was studying at university when I started going for longer and longer walks to help me think through my thoughts in more structured ways. I had a worry from a school experience that I was a homosexual and I don't know if it was a nervous breakdown or what, but I wanted to tell everyone. I felt great for a while about this, as if for the first time I was really facing life and 'bit back' with such a buzz. I sensed that things were a bit 'up in the air' for me and started to see a student counsellor who was very helpful and she referred me to a psychiatrist.

When I went home for the summer holidays I told my parents of all that had been going on for me - with the thinking that I was homosexual and all the psychiatric stuff. We were living down south at the time so my father came back up to Scotland with me to see the psychiatrist and I was referred to the hospital where I became an inpatient for a few months. At that point I really couldn't understand what it was all about. I remember being told that it was just like breaking your leg and all I needed to do was let it heal again. This didn't make sense to me as I thought 'I haven't broken my leg and I need a new shirt' so I walked about 3 miles into town to buy one. On my return to the ward they were all in a panic as they thought I had done a runner! I just didn't understand what it was all about.

After a few months in the hospital my dad came up and took me home. By this time I felt that life was quite hard but I was going to keep going at it and the only way I felt I could do so was to be quite direct about expressing myself. I suppose my behaviour was odd as I was so direct. As we grow older we find ways of 'going round' something rather than being so direct but I hadn't learnt that yet. It was as if I went too far all the time. Teenagers can be a bit boisterous going out on the town with friends, having a few drinks and clowning around but I was doing these things on my own, getting a buzz from it and taking life on or so I thought.

It was probably a couple of years before I was admitted to hospital again. I did realise that people my age would be training for a job or in a job and I realised that the way I was behaving was putting my family under strain so I took myself off for a holiday in Scotland. It was an enjoyable holiday but I still almost felt this duty to just talk to someone for a bit too long. I saw it as trying to get to the truth of the matter, to find a way for myself. I was genuinely trying to find something that I could relate to but I ended up in hospital again when I came home. I have been in a few hospitals while living down south, one was for nine months with some nice people and wards and so on but I don't have particularly good memories of the locked ward there.

My parents decided to move back to Edinburgh and I came with them. This was when things began to go badly for me. I was on a medicine which gave me these feelings like a chemical change in my body. I could feel it happening and all of a sudden I was in touch with my subconscious side. From anywhere between two and eight hours I would have these really bad feelings and it was very scary for me. I remember having flutters of these feelings previously but not full blown. By this time though these horrible feelings had taken a hold at least once a week and I thought these 'bad thoughts' made me a bad person. I still wanted to take part in life and the only way I could think to do so was to follow out the thoughts that were going on in my mind. So it wasn't too long before I ended up in the locked ward of the psychiatric hospital again.

To cut a long story short my behaviour became so worrying to me and the staff that I was transferred to the state hospital. To be honest I had quite a rough time there but once I 'played by the rules' type of thing, it became a bit easier for me. I was still getting the thoughts and responding so was restrained at times but overall I do think that there was a bad feeling to the place. Mostly the staff did try to help but it was in quite an unhelpful regime with some staff joking that they weren't nurses but prison wardens.

After a couple of years my medication was changed and all of a sudden these episodes, for want of a better word, suddenly stopped. All the thoughts stopped and I began to feel the buzz for life, that 'great to be alive' feeling again. When you are used to having, once a week, between two and eight hours of feeling like that, then all of a sudden it's gone-it is like a great weight lifted. After another year, it was decided that I didn't need to be there anymore and I was moved back to the hospital in Edinburgh. I couldn't quite believe coming back to Edinburgh again and appreciating my freedom while on the ward. Though I would question how helpful a hospital is as a place to get better when you are in such close proximity to other people who are also unwell.

I don't know if it was some slight change in my meds or a change in me but the tension episodes came back and I remember being on a different ward as my ward was full. I went back to bed to sort of hide away but one of the senior nurses came up to me, realising that I felt ill and asked if I wanted to talk about it. I said no and turned round in my bed. I was really thinking 'I have only been away from the state hospital for a matter of weeks and this is me going back there because I'm getting these feelings again.' It was something in the way she asked, 'do you want to talk?' that made an impression on me. So thinking that I've got to make the best of it and I didn't want to go back I started to talk about the feelings I was having. They were frightening but actually managing to talk about them was a good thing. The Royal Edinburgh was definitely a different 'kettle of fish' from the state hospital and people would make time to listen to me if I needed them to.

I was then moved to a rehabilitation ward in the old Queens Clinic where I was quite happy. I was really enjoying myself and finding the lovely grounds therapeutic. It was about a year later that I went on one of my 'escapades'. I was still sectioned under the 1984 Mental Health Act but I had learnt from reading my father's copy of the Act that there was this clause that said if a person absconds for 28 days the section is no longer in force. I wanted discharged but was on a section and medication so I thought a good idea for me was to abscond. I got myself all prepared in a matter of days writing letters to the hospital and my parents because I didn't feel I could tell anyone. I was so worried that people would be chasing after me, hunting me down, that I bought a wig and shaved my beard in toilets near the railway station before setting off up north. I fancied myself as a sort of lone figure walking through the Highlands with my rucksack, on the run as it were. When I got there I called my dad but thinking that there would be a bug on the phone I kept it really short. I was worried that they would find me by tracing my call. My dad answered and I just said, 'Hello, it's me, I'm absconding for 28 days to get out of hospital' and put the phone back down again. I realised that I was going to be too lonely up there so went to the opposite extreme and headed for London.

London, when I got there, I just thought was too dirty and crowded so looking at the departures lounge I saw there was a train leaving for Liverpool so that is where I went, staying in a YMCA for three weeks. I knew the medication would take three weeks to get out of my system and lo and behold after three weeks these feelings went away and I felt great again. I spent the last week back in London counting out the days until I had done my 28 days.

I always remember one day looking out of the windows of the YMCA in London and seeing all these London Bobbies rushing into the building and me desperately leafing through my notebook to see if I had done enough days but they come out with someone else! I was so relieved and also realised that 28 days had now passed so called my psychiatrist. I asked him if I was free and he replied 'oh yes, you are but I think you should call your mother.'

It was bad news. I learnt that my father had died whilst I was away. He and my sister had been hill walking on one of the Munros, Schiehallion, when he died of a sudden heart attack. It upset me more than I consciously felt at the time as you don't always feel like you think you would at the time when things like that happen.

I came back up to Edinburgh and got myself a flat with a landlady and I was off my section and my medications. Things were going quite well for me but after three or four months I was beginning to feel unwell again and was admitted back into the Queens Clinic – the one I absconded from.

One good thing was that the Psychiatrist realised that I had been really quite well off my medication and I stayed off them for about a year, year and a half. My sister died in 1988 after being diagnosed with cancer in '85 and I don't know if it was because of that but I became unwell again. I was put back on the medication that had caused me to have these horrible tension episodes so I had to battle not only with this again but losing my motivation as well. In time I was discharged into a hostel where I was for about five years. Every week or so I was getting these thoughts/episodes but, in a funny way, I was beginning to learn to be 'ok, this is what is happening to me but I'm not going to overreact to them. It is not a pleasant feeling, but I'm just going to sit in my chair or whatever but I'm not going to react.' So, in that way, these thoughts only went on for a matter of hours. I was fairly happy in the hostel, socialising with the other residents and staff but eventually I did become unwell again and was admitted to hospital where I was moved to a hospital hostel nearby.

In this hostel I was still having the same feeling and a friend, who I had met a few years ago in the hospital, told me about the difference a new medication was having on him and suggested I ask my doctor about it. I really didn't have much hope but the doctor agreed to try it. After three weeks of getting the old medication out of my system I felt great and I was about a year on this new medication. I wasn't really motivated but at least I wasn't getting the bad feelings. Then I caught the flu which meant I had to come off this medication – something to do with white blood cells. I was also hardly eating so it was a hard time for me and I was admitted back onto an acute ward. You could say that I really had my plate full yet I still managed to handle myself and put up with things the best I could. I was worried about what I could be in for as I was told that after having the flu you couldn't go on this medication again. The drug company thankfully decided that as so many people had flu that year that it would actually be alright for people to go back on the medication again. I remember the doctor coming to tell me this and I cried with relief, it was such a relief. I got my motivation back again and got back to the hostel. Everything was buzzing again and I felt great.

It was maybe a few months later that we were told that the hospital was going to close the hostel and the Multi-Agency Team (MAT) were going to help us find places in the community to live. I was shocked at first, everyone was. The MAT team were very helpful though and different. They put a bit of thought into it and tried to find what was right for me which was good. The first flats I saw were awfully small so I didn't think I wanted to stay there and eventually chose a shared flat in the New Town with a nice bunch of people including some from the hostel who moved at the same time. It was great there and I felt fairly motivated and very happy.

After about three years, my care manager talked with me about another move and she suggested a smaller shared house. The flat was still good but I needed a change and like all flat shares the time comes to move on. The new flat had less people and as I liked the company from a larger number of flatmates I wasn't too sure but I was looking forward to it. My care manager from the MAT team was really good. She was trying to find out what I wanted rather than just putting me somewhere for the sake of it which I found really considerate. Also being treated in such a considerate way was really nice. It all helped me to feel comfortable within myself.

So I moved again into a shared housing association flat with support from another organisation and was happy, though again like all flat shares, some things were beginning to niggle me.

A couple of years ago, my mother, who had always said that she would buy me my own flat suggested we start looking and that is where I am today. I still have visiting support from the same organisation which is helpful. Most of the time I am alright but they are there to just have a chat or offer to help with any housework but also if I'm feeling particularly down or under pressure for whatever reason I feel that I can really talk things through with the support workers which is really helpful. They call it person-centred support and they really do try and help you in the way you want to be helped and willing to listen if you have any difficulties with the support.

I feel quite good now. I have had a hard life but I've lived a good life and I still get a buzz out of being able to fit in with the rest of society. Being active and doing my own thing gives me a real buzz. Considering how difficult I've found just the process of living in the past it's good to find it relatively straightforward these days. It was important getting my own flat and I'm glad my mum pushed me because I wasn't sure the time was right for me. I have my flat, my gerbils and my cycling. I love the freedom of getting away, meeting people and seeing beautiful scenery. I go to things most of the week, either morning or afternoon to keep busy so that I can look forward to the weekend. My mum has since died but she was happy that I was settled and had my own home.

I think I have almost come full circle back to 'normality.' In all of my experiences, especially when I got my health back, I felt I was well treated. People helped me but I did have to do the hard work.

Learning that I didn't have to react to the thoughts and when I feel up to it doing the things that I really want to do all helped. By coming full circle I mean taking the bits of 'normality' that *you* have found yourself work and just leaving the others to one side. Living the life you want to live within society but not necessarily embracing every part but just the parts you want. The really bad experiences I had with two medicines still make me wonder if the drugs made me feel like that – are the problems they are causing actually worse than what they are meant to be putting right? I'm not sure at what point I realised it was a medication that was making me have those feelings. Otherwise I would say that the feelings aren't going to last forever and to just sit them out. Then, once they are over you can get on and do the things you want to do with the rest of your life. It's not worth over-reacting to feelings and talking about the feelings really helps. If you keep it to yourself it feels like it's your own fault but if you share them you realise that things are not all that bad. By taking control of myself rather than responding to these feelings has been a great lesson to learn.

As well treated as I have been recently, I would love to leave the psychiatric system completely and just be a citizen in my own right. I also think that with all the experiences I have been through I have learnt things that are worth sharing and if I could help people in some way with my experiences that would be good.

Coming full circle 31

Artist: Jeanette

I did it my way!

By Joan

I can't believe it, eight years I have been out of hospital but there you are, look at the difference. It's great! You can lead your life and not go into hospital.

I was fed up of going in and out of hospital anyway. I was well and staying in a hospital hostel where I met people and it was good. Then my care manager from the MAT (Multi Agency Team) said that they were going to get supported accommodation for us and we could live our own life. The hospital was going to rent the hostel to a support organisation and change it into a shared house where we would become tenants instead of patients so I decided to stay on. Support workers would support us instead of nursing staff. The hostel had been alright but it turned more into a home with the change over and we got new furniture which was great.

The new support workers were great, so reassuring and I enjoyed doing what I wanted. They took us out for coffees to be introduced to our key workers and the rest of the team as well which was really very good. I can go out for coffee myself but it helped getting to know them and they're all very good as I haven't had a dud yet! They are trained to support and things to help them understand and they said I did very well. My new key worker, Susie, was lovely and she helped me a lot though it's up to me to make a bit of an effort myself. You can't have all roses, life is not like that and the support workers do their best for you.

Jennifer, my care manager, was a nice person and helpful as well though I didn't always think so at the time. She also knew when I was turning not well, as she would say 'you are not your usual self today, what's wrong?' I was well but not as well as I am now.

Before, the hostel staff were quite strict. If you did certain things you were hospitalised and I didn't like that. When it changed to the support organisation I thought 'thank goodness, we will be able to do what we want, lead our own life.' Oh, I loved it and they took us a holiday in a car to Oban which was great. I enjoyed it but now I can experiment and go abroad and do whatever I want. I had been abroad before with my mother, so it wasn't new to me and I went to Jersey last year.

With the new support we also got Disability Living Allowance (DLA) though I had money in the bank anyway as I had worked in my life. I wasn't always so ill that I was in the hospital. I think I did not bad even though I say so myself and was glad I was able to work because some people haven't been able to.

At first, I needed a lot of support as I think I was a bit of a handful just didn't realise at the time. I used to worry a lot but I stopped it and that was when I was recovered. The support helps you on your feet and I was told I needed it so I took that on board. The support workers help you learn to cook and prepare you for going into your own place and you can do your own thing. They are only helping you, not interfering with your life or taking over. I needed a lot at first but now it's hardly any. In fact I've had support from the same organisation for eight years and I have my own flat now.

It's great having a home that is all my own. I knew someone else who moved into his own flat and I thought if he can do it then so can I. At first I didn't think I would be able cope on my own because I like company but then I also like my own company sometimes as well. When you are sharing in a house you have got to understand everyone's ways. I got on fine with everyone but they were all men but it would have been nice to have had another woman. Ultimately I didn't want to live with other people, not really, and it's nice having my own home.

Last year, somebody said that there were houses for sale up here and they had a warden. First come, first served so I was quick and got my house. My mother had died and I got a good price for our house which meant I could afford to buy.

It was exciting moving into my new home, getting new furniture and my key worker helped me. I've been very lucky as all my key workers have been great. We went to Ikea first but it would have been too much to carry so we just scrapped it and tried John Lewis which is where I got everything. It's nice being able to talk about it as it is a step on. I was so happy because in one year I had a holiday and a new home – it was great!

Now I have a new care manager but I never see him apart from a review and all that. I think the reviews are a waste of time but I suppose they aren't. I've also got a Community Psychiatric Nurse (CPN) who comes once a fortnight and is very nice. I thought I would like a CPN because they know about the illness.

I am very happy as well so I think that makes a difference. I have been well since my 50s, so that's 12 years that I've been well which is good. I just did it and I felt better. Before, I was always worrying, getting myself ill.

Previously the nurses were always saying 'get occupied, get occupied' that is more or less what they told you in the hospital. So I thought I'm going to enjoy myself, not going to waste it getting ill, so I did! When we were in hospital, we made toast for our tea, cheese on toast. We were occupied doing our own washing and going for coffees which were good. I used to worry all the time though and make myself ill though these days are over and I wouldn't do that now. I just said that I'm not going to worry about things and that will help me so I will be happier. I also keep active and just get on with my life. I go to Church, the day centre and college, but I will soon be 70 so I will be retiring from college as I don't want to go on for longer than 70. I've studied music but I'm going to do it again as well as Scotland's Politics. I've enjoyed it but it's time to give someone else a shot. When you have your own house you keep quite busy anyway.

I also play the keyboard and sing as well as just getting on with things in the house. At the time when my mother wasn't well I made her tea and did her shopping but I wasn't really able to look after her but I went down every night to see her. She has been dead about three years but she lived to be 93 which was a good age. She also stayed in a Care Home where they were very good to her. It was quite expensive but it was worth it, as it meant I could live my life. It was sad knowing that she wasn't going to get any better but they looked after her.

I think I would still be going in and out of hospital if it wasn't for my support workers. If I was going to go down to get the Psychiatric Emergency Team (PET) I would say 'I hope they don't take me in, I don't want to go in.' They were so reassuring, saying that I wasn't ill enough which was awfully good.

How I look on it, you see people getting on with their lives and although I have had mental health problems I can hear, I can see, I can do all the things I need. There are people worse off than me and that is how I look on it. Positive thinking, I learnt that from the hospital, 'positive thinking, positive thinking!'

I do more of my own thing now. I have a good friend that I've known for 60 years. I'm also going on holiday to Barcelona. My support workers come and see me here in my flat in the morning and we have a chat and then they go away and come back again in the evening but that's all. It's nice to get a wee bit company to talk to. They are not doing as much now as at first because then I wasn't so well and I sometimes needed more support, 24 hours at first. A big change!

I don't need to be in hospital but if I had to I wouldn't worry because I went to see the ward and it was a nice ward. They're not keeping you so much in hospital now. The days when they did I hated it. Oh no, I couldn't spend my life in that place again as it would drive me nuts, all the rules and regulations. They are not so strict now I believe. In the past, in the other ward, they were strict but they got me better. Well, I helped myself. I did it!

They used to say in the hospital 'Cheer up, there is always light at the end of the tunnel, that there's always a happy ending, it won't go on for ever' but I didn't believe it.

I got fed up of going in and out of hospital and now I have my life, there is light at the end of the tunnel and it's great. It was up to me to stop it and I did!

I did it my way! 37

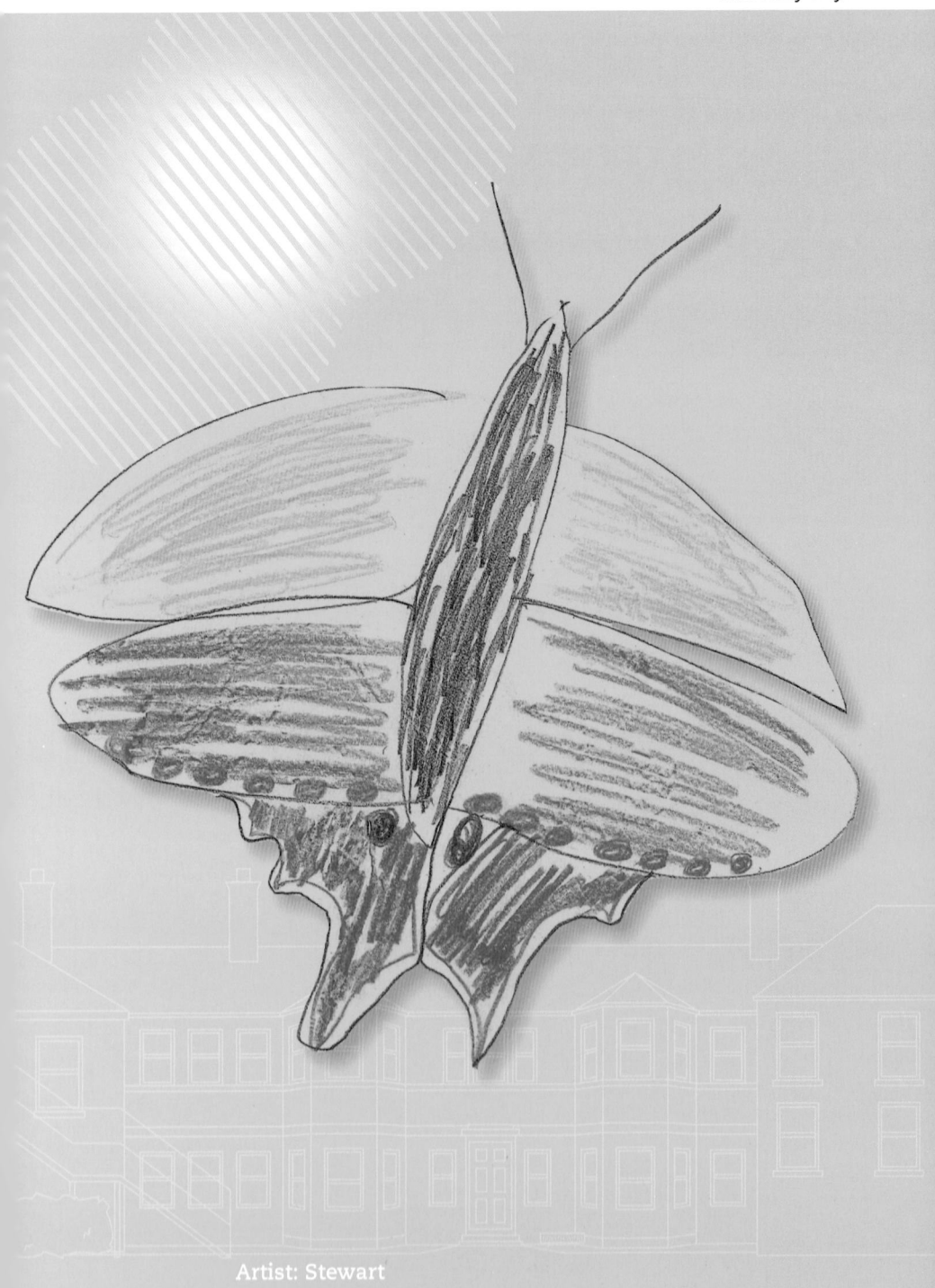

Artist: Stewart

Recovering in the community

By James W. Brown

William Shakespeare said that there were seven ages of man. In your twenties you are in soldier stage though I can't remember it exactly but I've reached a peaceful stage in my life where I am at peace with things and that has helped. My life has changed dramatically since I moved out of hospital which has mainly been a good experience.

I'm glad that I have got friends from outside my mental health experiences who still take me seriously and like me. I also feel quite lucky to have the support around me that I do have as I know how difficult life can be. Sometimes when I see some of the people who spend all of their lives in the hospital and their lives revolve around the hospital it does make me think…

When I moved out of the hospital I felt that everybody agreed. I moved in with my friend and another girl and we had a fairly good time. My doctor agreed with the discharge plan I had drawn up with my care manager and friends. I also met another woman who is still a very good friend of mine. After a time, my friend and I moved into our own place. Unfortunately he became unwell and I wasn't well enough to look after him so I got offered the flat I'm in now. It was bare but I had some money to spend so I was able to personally design the interior and stayed up late with Ikea and Argos catalogues planning. It felt like a new beginning for me as I didn't really feel a part of society so having my own flat, money and having a sense of purpose to be stronger has meant a big change for me. I now feel stronger, part of society and free. I have ways to manage for the times when I'm not always in the right state to be stronger.

I rent my flat from a housing association and my support is separate from a support organisation, so I could change my support if I wanted to but it's good just now. I have contact with most of the team even though they are busy with lots of new work though they tend to do what my care manager tells them, not always what I ask them to do! If I ever need to speak to them, they are just on the end of a telephone, they know me and I know them. It's good and I would say it works for me though they are very overworked. The support system is not how I would design it but I try to be a pragmatist and work within it and I do find them helpful. If I was designing a support service it would be a lot more laid back and person-centred.

I'm really a pretty sociable person and don't find it difficult to make friends, never have done. I have long term and short term friends. I found knowing people and making friends with people who hadn't been involved in the Mental Health system did me a lot of good as well as the supports from my care manager who works with the Community Rehabilitation Team (CRT) and my doctor. I also have support from various support agencies and I'm doing ok now. I get on with my care manager who I like a lot and he is very good at what he does. He has a 'hands on' approach and doesn't shrink from difficult situations. I tend to get on with health professionals and don't think I would be where I am at the moment if I didn't, I can say that for sure. I have the trust of my support people and they don't think that I am a risk to be outside in the community which I think some people must think of people like me, 'being a bit mad' and all that. It's a horrible feeling.

Moving here to my own flat meant I had a comfortable place where I could wash my clothes, have deep baths, keep the place reasonably tidy and everything was new. It's absolutely great compared to being in some of the places I have been including a locked ward. When my brother came up to see my flat, he jokingly said 'Ah, now I see what my tax money is wasted on' – think he was impressed with my interior designing! My rent is very low being a Housing Association flat so I can afford to go out to work though I can't imagine myself doing anything that great at the moment. Apparently I have to get a job which is something which I am not looking forward to just now. I may not have a job, do voluntary work or anything like that at the moment but I don't feel that I am a negative effect on society. To be honest I feel I just lost out on education though I think I have matured like a fine wine! Life is a certainly one big learning curve.

For a while I was spending so much time in pubs that it explains how I got my alcohol problem and it was where I would spend all my money. My friends were in pubs so that was where I used to hang out. It was a horrible way to be, propping up the bar every day. I was slow, half drunk all the time and putting on loads of weight. It was awful and I am glad in a way that my money is controlled at the moment. I am on Incapax where I get an agreed amount of my money each day and I now keep away from pubs.

To be honest I found it awful being in hospital as you begin to think that the way they are treating you is right but it is so obviously wrong. When I was first admitted to the Intensive Psychiatric Care Unit (IPCU) I had never experienced anything like it, I was just really shocked. When I moved to the rehabilitation ward I found it helpful as I knew I needed to sort myself out. I guess you need to have faith in yourself as sometimes it was difficult. I also had a relationship with a woman while there which was good, really nice. When you go into hospital it's to get away from some things but it can actually magnify them and make them worse. I do feel a bit mentally scarred from being in hospital. I felt that some staff tried to make me out to be some things, so I had to keep on good form so that I could defend myself mentally which was a bit difficult.

I have good family support. My parents stay in Edinburgh and I stay there some Saturday nights and get a good meal. I also see my nephews and my brother maybe three or four times a year when they come up. Both my parents still work though my dad retires this year. I joke that I could give him lessons about doing nothing (as I sit and smoke most of the time but I *love* cigarettes!) Doing nothing is my favourite pastime, it is fantastic. I am joking though I think my dad will find it difficult without his work.

The support from the CRT is pretty good too, as when I become unwell, I don't have to go to one of the sector wards, I go to the Rehab ward which is far better. It has moved recently and is so much better as the old ward was pretty horrible. They also used to wake you up at 8am and I didn't like it at the time. I've been deprived of most things at some time in my life and the thing that has affected me the most is being deprived of sleep so every time I lie down I think 'this is a luxury.' It did me good in the long run though as it made me think about the things that people take for granted and if I had a job I would probably have to get up at 8am.

I also have a Mental Health Officer (MHO) at the moment as I am on a Compulsory Treatment Order – that's just to make sure that I do all the things that are expected of me. He is also a kind of mental health crusader which I find a bit strange but good that he is in the business of being a MHO when he has got some pretty liberal views. I had a lovely woman who was my MHO when I first went into hospital and when I met her ten years later she still remembered me. There was also this other MHO who I just didn't feel he wanted to listen to me as he kept on saying 'listen, you can say what you want but I still get paid' whereas my present one does and is happy to chat with me, he is very different.

I enjoy talking to people and am very sociable. It is good to come out of hospital and to take the positive things with you and leave the bad things behind. I mean it hasn't got me working or anything yet but it still is beneficial. I've worked for quite a few projects but I didn't really feel stimulated. One of the reasons that I went into hospital was because I couldn't compete. I lost everything in my life but I'm getting things back now and I want to be able to make a difference. I have been encouraged to do Focus work with the support organisation and the guy who runs it is really nice. It's all about involvement and will be great if I can do it, building on my confidence and helping out.

I just hope that in some way I can live a good life and hopefully be an inspiration to people who are finding life difficult. My life is ok now, not great but I suppose that depends on what you wish for.

Recovering in the community 43

Artist: Phyllis

My home is where my heart is

By Norman

My health, since I came out of hospital, has improved remarkably. I used to get voices and things but the doctors said that the voices were there because of a stress-related illness. I had been under a lot of stress at the time so I was diagnosed with schizophrenia and I took it from there. I have been on various medications and am now happy with the combination I take. I sleep really well on the tablets as they help me completely relax.

I used to work for BT and really enjoyed my job. At first I worked as a clerical assistant then I was put in the relief team which meant I had to be able to drive. Luckily I had a licence and really enjoyed driving. In 1980, I was staying with my parents, when they knew something was wrong with me. My neighbour helped get access to the doctor as it was in the evening so I ended up seeing the duty psychiatrist at the hospital and was admitted to an acute ward.

I was discharged after nine months and went back to work with BT though doing a different job but I couldn't keep up with the work. When the work said I would have to go, I says 'right, then how do I stand pension wise sir?' I was told I would get a pension of £10 a week. I says 'alright' and went to work in the hospital on the gardening course. I still get my pension and it's worth £132.12 a month today which is good because I can really enjoy myself with that and make it work for me.

I really liked the freedom of the gardening, working with plants. I was there for 17 years then I went to another project that built on my clerical skills and I was there for five years. One of my jobs there was sending out over 3000 leaflets a year to all the conferences that came to Edinburgh. Today I am working in a social firm which I enjoy and get on remarkably well with the other staff. I work in the delicatessen part of the bakery where they work the bread and there is a café upstairs. It's an early start but I am a morning person and I like working in the mornings as opposed to the afternoon. I get up at 7am every morning, have my breakfast and make my way over to the bakery as I work from 9am-1pm. I would really like to work as a lollipop man when I move on from the bakery. I am planning a move now, branching out into something completely new for me and I'm really looking forward to it. My father was really good as a lollipop man and I want to do as well as him.

In total I have spent a long time in hospital. I was ten years on an acute ward followed by five years on a rehabilitation ward and I've now been here five years. I moved here when Eleanor Adams (from the support organisation) came to visit me in the rehab ward. It was the first time I heard about the hope of moving out of hospital. I was offered a flat in a building with support workers 24 hours a day. At first I visited on a Sunday and stayed over, then stayed every Wednesday and Sunday for a month before finally moving in. I inherited my furniture when I moved in and the only things I had to buy were my microwave and stereo. It was really interesting how I managed to motivate myself to move. I prayed saying 'God, if you give me this flat, I'll live for you' and I had also said to my mum that I would give it a go and I was successful!

It was an uplifting experience moving here and I really feel the difference. I was very quiet on the ward but I'm not today. When I was on the acute ward it was horrendous, but my consultant guided me through it and she sort of followed me when I moved to the rehab ward where I was for five years. Now I've got my flat I get on better with my parents, which is good. My dad is now in a nursing home so I feel an extra responsibility. I feel safe in my flat as no-one is going to break in and steal my stuff, not like in the hospital. I found that my first consultant psychiatrist, Anne, was very homely, then Caroline, who was a good guide. Now I have another consultant, Dr Barron, who I see every three months in the clinic. I think he will probably find it more helpful than me as it's his job to find out how I'm doing. He can learn from me since I am so successful!

I've really settled in here in my flat, being my own boss and doing things for myself. At first I had a care manager, Mary Jones, from the Community Rehab Team (CRT) and she came to see me every Wednesday for six months until I was established then Louise took over but now I have Sarah Brown who only comes down every six months for a review here in my flat. I find reviews helpful as I talk about my progress and how I'm getting on. They prove to me that someone is looking out for me. I have never had any problems here as Paul and Robbie are in charge, which I like. We all have our own flats and there is a big sitting room downstairs where we have get togethers and celebrations like birthdays – I'll be 50 in June! I have my dignity, security and feel safe which I value. I get on with everyone and enjoy every minute which suits me.

Financially, after I have paid all my bills, I am left with £40 a week to buy CDs, clothes and my food. I also have my pension and £10 a week from my work in the bakery.

Fred is my care worker here. I was asked if I would like him as my keyworker and I do everything with him. I also have a support agreement that gives me the freedom to do what I want. This support organisation is good and I have been to their Annual General Meetings, local forums and also taking part in training for staff. I really enjoyed these experiences and have now been asked to be part of the working group for the forums.

I also do my own things and having a bus pass means I can get a care worker on the bus with me, which is good. I have been all around Scotland and to Brussels on holiday with a friend, who also stayed here, and some support staff so I've been quite varied in what I've done. My friend has now moved into a new flat with more independence and we hope to still meet up. I used to love driving but I had to give up my licence when I was put on a new medication years ago on the acute ward. My consultant, Caroline, asked me if I had my licence as she was sorry but I would have to hand it over. I asked her if I could get a bus pass instead and she arranged for me to get one. I also enjoy walking though I don't really have the time just now with my job. I used to belong to a walking group and one time we went on the Glentress Walk in Peebles but it was chucking it down so we were glad to get back on the bus out of the rain!

I am so happy here and looking forward to my future. I've learned that you can be all that you need to be and that by doing what I could I settled down and have a good life.

Getting my life back!

By Mary

Life is great now and yes I can say that I am recovered! I'm amazed at what I do; going to the gym, the theatre, spending time with family and friends as well as being involved with the Patients' Council. I have achieved so much compared to when I was first admitted to hospital. It is a complete turnaround and I am very comfortable now with life.

I don't remember much about going into hospital the first time as it's all a bit of a blank. I was being treated by my GP because I didn't want to be referred to a psychiatrist but the time came when I needed to be. He admitted me to hospital where I remember going onto the acute ward feeling very frightened and restless. Over a number of years I became what can be referred to as a 'revolving door' patient with the longest time I spent as an inpatient being a year.

After about four years my consultant asked if I would like to move to a new rehabilitation ward that was being opened. I didn't think I needed rehabilitating and told him so! The consultant for this new ward also came and spoke to me and I told her the same. Over the next few days, when everyone had left me, I thought maybe going to this ward would be the only way for me to stay out of hospital for good so I said that I would go. I remember the look on my consultant's face, kind of exasperated, but he said that this rehab ward could offer me a lot more than he could.

Unfortunately, around the same time, I broke my ankle and developed MRSA and was moved to a general hospital to recover. It was also at this time that the acute ward I had been on was converted into this new rehab ward. By the time I returned everyone was new to me and I found it difficult to cope with the changes. I felt abandoned as the people I knew, both staff and patients, had moved. I don't remember much except for the room I had with the wallpaper coming off the walls and some of the new staff.

I met Jane on this ward who became my care manager. Jane was from the Multi-Agency Team (MAT) and when she first came to see me on the ward she offered to take me into Morningside. I remember being very tearful as I couldn't stand the noise or the number of people. Jane also came back to my home with me and I remember feeling it was like a hotel, as if I didn't live there. I wondered how I could ever have felt comfortable there and amazed that I had even used the kitchen to cook food. It felt so unreal and the amount of mail I had was overwhelming. Fortunately my bills were paid by direct debit so I didn't have any 'red' letters demanding payment. Jane sat with me as I worked my way through every one. Looking back, I feel that by being on the acute ward for so long, I became completely de-skilled and I just didn't know how to manage life for myself.

Yet so much is different now. I think the change began by being able to trust people in the rehab ward. They worked as a team and were clear that there was no rush and I could take as long as I needed. Everything I did was in small, manageable steps and they supported me all the way. The staff emphasised that they were a team of people and I felt included which was very person-centred. Slowly I was building up the confidence that I had completely lost. My time on this ward was very different to previously on the acute ward. Then it felt as if one person made all the decisions and you were lucky if you were even called into a ward round. I felt that I was acting a part, the role being that of a patient with the staff either learning about or from my behaviour. My new consultant became someone I could trust. I do remember not being very happy in the beginning as she seemed, to me, a very formidable lady! I trust her now to make the right decisions with and for me, balancing my safety and managing risk. Our relationship is so different and I find that she is both supportive and not too restrictive.

Jane is still my care manager though she now works with the CRT team. It has been good to have this continuity as she is supportive and knows me quite well. I have met others from the CRT team and they are always very pleasant which really makes a difference. Their approach is one where nothing is rushed, everything will be sorted and 'we are always here'. It has been helpful to take these very small steps that I needed to take and that they also took the time to get to know me. Yes, on the acute ward the consultant knew me, the staff knew me, it was just that I didn't feel there was any real engagement. Whereas my experiences with the MAT, CRT and rehab teams I felt absolutely engaged as their approach is very holistic and I feel listened to. Having someone interested in me as a person rather than just being seen as a patient has made such a difference. I remember thinking on the acute ward that there was a patient who was very lucky because their keyworker would actually talk with them. I don't think I ever had a keyworker there who actually sat down with me and asked if we could have a chat and catch up.

My life became so much better as I gained in confidence. I was discharged with both a Care Plan and a support package. I'm not sure whether I had a Care Plan or not on the acute ward as it was never discussed with me, more 'this is what is going to happen'. Now my Care Plan is reviewed every six months and having the support workers, from another organisation, is very good. To be honest, I really resented the support at first but now find their support very good. My team is small and made up of people who know me really well which is really important to me. I can rely on them and they will always let me know if someone is unable to come or come if I ask them to. All in all I have a very well thought out support package that is focused on practical issues so that I don't end up getting overwhelmed and feeling as if I can't cope.

Through my work with the Patients' Council I was at a workshop recently where I heard that a person may have 24 hour support in the community to begin with but that there may come a time when they don't need that support anymore. I can't see that happening for me just yet but it's good that people are realising how support is an essential part of people's recovery. It definitely has been for me as without the support I have had I would either not be here or still in hospital. With friends and family I am always conscious not to talk about myself let alone my feelings, yet with support workers, even though 90 per cent of the time I don't talk about myself, I know that I can, that they will listen and there will be no judgements made. Sometimes, with family, if I don't feel so great or I say to the children how I actually feel they immediately pick up on it and they worry when really I'm not that bad. In all, I now have the independence that I couldn't possibly have imagined a few years ago.

I have reviews which involve everyone in my support. This is important to me as it is a time for us all to get together and discuss what is happening and how things are going. I feel supported and in control as any problems I have can be brought up, discussed, sorted out and any changes can be agreed straight away. One person on the team who I have found really helpful is the pharmacist. As a 'secondary prescriber' she can, within limits, make changes to my medication though the big decisions are still made by my consultant. I can also phone up Jane any time I have a problem and we can get things sorted out.

I am presently on a CTO (Compulsory Treatment Order, community based) which means that I have a tribunal every two years. When I attended my first tribunal I was given a handbook which described what would happen and had a picture of people sitting around a table with a cup of coffee but that wasn't my experience. I felt upset when I heard all the professionals talking about me. I told the chairperson of the panel that I hadn't expected such an adversarial setting but his response, I felt, was dismissive. I had tried to evidence to the psychiatrist that I was better but I felt upset by the whole experience especially as my CTO was continued. My next tribunal I wrote saying that I didn't want go through a similar experience and I got a really horrible response back. At that tribunal though it was a different panel and my letters were included and read out. This meant that it was recorded that I felt that I hadn't been answered properly. Apparently this is important as it means the process and the people contributing are accountable, even psychiatrists! I just felt it was a waste of time and haven't bothered appealing since though maybe next time I will and get myself an advocate for support.

My one real objection about my CTO is that my Mental Health Officer (MHO) is meant to be independent and provide a second opinion but she will only meet with me for about five minutes so I feel that she doesn't really know me. I have asked her about this but she says that 'I get feedback from the team' so she doesn't think she needs to. I think she does as I feel that she knows more about me from others, especially when her opinion is sought regarding whether I remain on a CTO or not. I feel it is slightly disempowering that she would go to Jane rather than get to know me. I have reached a stage now that unless my CTO really encroaches on my life then I won't make a fuss. I trust my consultant and believe that she wouldn't admit to hospital lightly and there would have to be a good reason. Trust is very important to me and I'm glad that I have that now with everyone in my support.

Since my discharge I have been admitted a few times to hospital when I have had a difficult period. There is an arrangement that I get admitted to the rehab ward which is good as I have built up good relationships with the staff there and they are supportive. I'd be there for a few days then home again. I really think that the less time in hospital the better. It is so easy to become comfortable and forget how nice it is to be at home. The feeling of 'gosh, how long have I got to stay here?' can go in a matter of weeks and its easy to lose sight of how much better it is at home.

My experiences have led me to think there should be more emphasis in the hospital to get people to realise that it is a hospital and that it can't really replace home. I think there should be more emphasis on people having an illness that can be treated or controlled with the future always held as near as possible to your life outside the hospital. I was working when I was first admitted so if everything had been a lot shorter and I had been able to slip back into my life again it would have been a lot easier. Obviously the longer I was in hospital the more I thought I couldn't do a good job. It had been hard going for me before being admitted and I was getting in to quite a mess yet if I had been supported more at home and with my work I think I would have had an easier time. Yet what I am doing now and the confidence I have gained is encouraging and rewarding. I would never have thought six yeas ago that I would be able to sit on the committees and planning groups that I do with the Patients' Council. The hospital is going through a development just now and it is exciting both for me and to see that the nurses are as excited as me by it. I am finding the whole experience so rewarding. I think that any volunteering project would have been helpful just that, for me, it has been the Patients' Council. I have branched out onto other committees and working groups as I have gained in confidence and my interest has been stimulated. I have also found the supportive environment of the Horticultural Project in the grounds of the hospital very useful. I wasn't too sure at first that I liked the idea of gardening or weeding but they are so good at encouraging people to do what they want, what they are interested in and I now go twice a week. Sometimes though I do get quite tired with all I am involved with but I have learned to balance my life and commitments. What I have learnt about myself is that I don't respond very well to stress so I find ways to reduce this. Sometimes it is an effort and I have to make positive decisions if I feel myself going back into a shell again. If I haven't contacted people for a while then I make an effort to do so as it is very tempting to just shut the curtains and turn off the phone but that is the start of a slippery slope downwards for me. It is also important for me to really have a balance between my life and my involvement with the Patients' Council. If I have a number of meetings then I am very conscious that I need a counterbalance as it is so easy when I'm busy to let other things go. Therefore it is important for me to step back and do some of the things I enjoy.

I still feel the stigma of mental illness and I don't feel that I could speak to my friends about it or even about my work with the Patients' Council. They know I am busy and they refer to it but it is though it is a threatening world for them so we don't really discuss it. I am past the stage though of feeling the odd one out in a group because I have a mental health problem. I don't really see this as a problem anymore and have picked up my life where I left it before I first went into hospital. One of my friends did say 'oh, we have the old Mary back'. I have also made some good friends through the Patients' Council as it is a good peer group, especially when we see changes and achievements through our work. One achievement that stands out for me has been the improvements to the rehab ward. I did have a vested interest because if I ever have to be admitted again I know that it will now be to a better environment due to changes, improvements and the eviction of the resident mouse!

My life is so good now and I get so much enjoyment from my grandchildren and family. I remember being upset when one of my grandchildren thought that the hospital was my home. She was only four and didn't understand but it affected me. I needed to get my life back and now I have. We all visit each other regularly and I love having them come to my home. I didn't think I would be able to cope when I was first discharged but I have done and had great support in making this a reality.

A complete turnaround!

'Treat people as if they were what they ought to be, and help them become what they are capable of being.'

Goethe

'Relate to a person's potential and you call forth greatness'

Ike Powell

Reflections

'Working with, and being part of some of the most wonderful changes from patients to people, was an absolute honour.' Nicole LeBlond (former Link Living)

'It was the hardest and the most rewarding job I've ever done. The way our team worked was radically different to the rest of the hospital which brought many challenges each day as we chartered unknown territory. The strong values and commitment from the team, along with the determination of the people we worked with, made me realise that anything really is possible.' Kelly Nicol (former MAT)

'Change can be exciting but can be like walking into a room with no lights on! As Clinical Services Manager, I always felt it was so strange for a supportive, caring organisation to allow people no rights and exclude them from planning after forcing them to stay (for many years) and not building confidence and self-reliance. It is a great privilege to be alongside people at times of change hopefully helping them turn on some lights. Person-centred planning is key to this way of working with people.' Paul Pacey

'The most rewarding aspect of our jobs is to see how people make the sort of changes to their lives that allow them to progress in spite of some of the difficulties they have. At times it can be challenging to keep hope alive when some situations feel hopeless. In these circumstances, it is focusing and building on strengths that provide the way forward, while acknowledging and managing current problems. It is often humbling to witness the work and effort that people make to overcome their obstacles.'
Debbie Mountain (Consultant Psychiatrist)

'In the first wave of re-provisioning I was working as a support worker with people who were moving out of hospital which was exciting and it was a privilege to be part of people's lives at a time of major change. It was fantastic to see how people's lives expanded in so many different ways when they moved into their own homes and were in control of their lives.

As I really enjoy helping people think through how they would like their lives to be and working towards making it a reality I pursued my interest in this area and after training as a social worker I am now working with the CRT team which brings me back into contact with some of the people I supported.

It's fantastic to see people grow in confidence and take on things they never thought they would be able to and to continue to work with people through the challenges they may come up against.' Cathy Carpenter

'It is so inspiring to see people who never felt they could have a home of their own move out of hospital and flourish with the right environment.' Fiona

'What struck me most at the time that we set up our new service, and people began to move into their own homes having spent most of their adult lives in hospital, was the willingness of all involved to believe it would be a success. The service users embraced the opportunity to live in their own homes, become part of the community and start doing the things they had long wished for. It was often not huge things that marked out theses goals, but the small ones, taking control of their money, having private space and control over their time and how they used it. It has been a joy to watch people take control of their lives, develop friendships, get married, do new things and visit new places.' Andy Egerton (Places for People)

Creating a desirable future

By Susan McMeel

In reflecting on my work with people as part of the Multi-Agency Team, initially the prospect of nearly 100 people being able to set up new homes and leave hospital was both daunting and exciting. Lack of suitable housing had previously been one of the obstacles for people leaving hospital along with after-care which did not always match what people needed and wanted. This was our chance to create new support services around people with an unprecedented choice of housing.

In order to figure out how people would like to live and then where this could be, we asked about the people, places and routines which were most important. We spent a lot of time not only with the person themselves but with other people who knew them well. We wrote down what people liked about the person and the stories that illustrated that person's good points and strengths. I was struck by the many talents and acts of kindness and friendship which these stories revealed. The new housing opportunities meant that moving with or near to friends from hospital or living near Morningside were possibilities.

There were worries and concerns as people who had been central to the care of inpatients for many years, including healthcare professionals, relatives and other carers, were anxious about people being discharged to the community, commonly after being in hospital for a long time. One theme was that carers and healthcare staff could not envisage or did not have confidence in how new social care providers could meet people's needs in a community setting. They doubted social care providers' ability to look after people as well as the hospital staff had done.

Bed closures were part of the re-provisioning programme and some people worried that if discharge arrangements did not work out there would be far fewer hospital beds to return to. The closure plans for hostels and wards, along with readiness of new housing, meant we had time pressures, setbacks and constraints to work through. I think a mixture of perseverance, hopeful attitudes and robust relationships led to greater confidence that people would thrive in their new environments and that the stress of taking such a big step into the unknown would be worth it.

It was worth it as we can see what worked well. As people began to move on, their positive stories inspired others to contemplate change: 'I've just seen Jimmy's flat – it's great and he's looking so well.' People still in hospital were encouraged and felt more hopeful about working through their own difficulties and having a better life ahead.

People made changes to their lives by building on what they were good at and finding their own ways of staying well and coping with stressful events. I admire the many people who have tried things beyond their previous comfort zone and accomplished personal goals and ambitions in travel, sport, employment, art and music. Shared interests have led to more equal relationships emerging with support staff and many people have found ways of reconnecting with their families again. I found that as relationships with healthcare professionals gained a more equal footing we could think more creatively with people about what we should and shouldn't do.

It is very rewarding to be involved in helping people figure out what works well for them and being part of creating a desirable future for people in the longer-stay wards. The people who we worked with in the Multi-Agency Team have moved on in their lives and have thrived on having a place of their own to call home. Despite living still with illness symptoms, practical and emotional difficulties, people tell us about how their new way of life and valued relationships enables them to feel they are in a better place.

I can see that, perhaps over several years, people have got to know and understand themselves better and have developed ways of asking for what they want and need from other people as well as more confidence in doing things for themselves.

Person-Centred Planning

Taken from Realising Recovery Module 4

By starting with the individual and viewing the world from their perspective.

> 'Climbing into their skin and walking around in it.'
> *To Kill a Mockingbird* by Harper Lee

Person-centred support is about helping people work out what they want, and person-centred approaches focus on how this is delivered.

Person-centred planning tools provide the basis for, and promote, ways of commissioning, organising and providing services grounded in listening to what people want. They are based on principles of rights, strengths, independence, choice and inclusion.

Reflections from Julie Heggie

'Using person-centred planning as a tool to help people think about moving out of hospital felt good – it felt as if people were really being listened to.'

> 'Services were designed around people and what they wanted and needed, rather than trying to fit people into existing services.'

'The people who lived in hostels and their relatives often said, "it's the first time I have been asked my opinion".'

> 'When developing a Person-Centred Plan with someone, you really felt as if you got to know the person, rather than a list of "needs".'

'I felt really good when people's lives became so full with "living" that they didn't need us any more.'

'Let people who would teach us remember this – we have minds of our own. We have dignity.'

(Unknown source)

By Jennifer Simpson

Involved in hospital closure programmes for approximately 20 years I have seen re-provisioning from a number of different roles, as an NHS employee and also a manager of voluntary sector services. Many things have changed or come in and out of fashion during this period, but the sense of commitment and privilege I feel, working to help people move after many years in hospital, is reinforced time and again when I see people make this life changing step.

I was involved in the first 'Support and Accommodation' project commissioned as part of the REH reprovisioning. There were many 'firsts' associated with this project as the boundaries and realities of 'partnership working' were tested and gradually understood. Along with this, the tenants' confidence was nurtured and slowly strengthened. Tiny shoots of individual achievement began to develop and were celebrated. Challenges which recurred for everyone were about role and relationship; with new partners, different teams and organisations as well as service users. How to develop and maintain a role which promoted independence and didn't hold artificial limitations in place?

I managed the project for over five years and my memories are of intense and demanding work which provided the deepest satisfaction and sense of achievement. I am humbled to have been present or part of momentous or pivotal events; part of the journey people made in their recovery. I have seen someone cry with joy opening a letter from their in-laws and son with whom they had lost contact with for many years. I helped someone buy their own car. Laughed with my team about the 'emergency call' because the light in the fridge kept going out! I have also stood by a coffin with a keyworker and flatmate; united by our sadness. I helped someone plan a five star trip to London to see Chelsea play Man United and met people returning from holiday to realise other passengers were greeting them by their name.

Each and every person we supported has found their way through life experiences I would have found intolerable. Now they are leading a life; participating in it, being challenged by it and finding ways to carry on, whilst also finding out more about themselves.

Personal growth is what happens for everyone if you are able to take risks as with leaving the seemingly safe, known boundaries of hospital behind and working in the space created as new roles and relationships develop and are explored.

The next step on my own journey was to return to the NHS as an Occupational Therapist, preparing people for discharge by helping them develop enough self confidence and preparing them more fully to take the risk and step out of hospital. I believe with conviction that the best service we can offer is to stand at the door and point the way out.

Morningside and beyond

By Terry O'Malley

I was the charge nurse of the hospital hostels at the time of the re-provisioning of the rehabilitation services in the Royal Edinburgh Hospital. As the aim of the re-provisioning was to actively support people to live in their own homes and communities rather than the accepted long term hospital care, many changes were therefore necessary. With people moving into their new homes, support was provided by a range of supported living organisations which gave rise to opportunities for nursing staff, including myself, to skill share and it was at this point that I experienced true joint working between healthcare and social care staff. The Multi-Agency Team (MAT) was pivotal during this time and the face-to-face working with all the providers/partners was both challenging and exciting!

Supporting people through this huge change process was about being responsive to their needs. For some people, engagement with this process was easier and they were making positive and informed choices about their future while others, who had spent a great deal of their adult life in hospital care, found this more of a challenge, so we worked with this and altered the pace of support and transition.

Many people expressed a wish to stay in the Morningside area so we responded to this by changing how we used the hostels the Royal Edinburgh Hospital already had in the area, which, at the time, provided rehabilitation services to around 34 people. The aim was to create shared living houses from the hostels, which would then be rented from the NHS thus giving the people who would stay there a different relationship with the NHS. They would no longer be patients but tenants, with full tenancy rights, and a supported living organisation would provide the support that individuals required. For other people, their wish was to move out of the Morningside area, and so other opportunities were created throughout the city. A variety of living options enabled this to happen, from large shared houses, shared and individual flats, all with support from a variety of support organisations.

I found the pace of people moving from hospital life to community life was done in a way that was as sensitive and responsive as possible, ensuring that we also involved carers and relatives as much as possible as we saw their involvement as fundamental and actively encouraged it.

For people who lived in the hostels at the time, the changes meant that they could have the advantage of staying together if they wanted and if they didn't, there were other options. This did mean that for a period some people had to move back into the hospital but their resettlement plans very much remained ongoing and they subsequently moved into accommodation that met their choices at the time.

In all, this was a huge exercise for everyone involved that gave opportunities for true joint working. The proposed closure of the hostels encouraged a 'more focused' approach to the ongoing rehabilitation work that the hospital already provided. By working individually with people and their carers we supported their involvement and encouraged people in making informed choices about their future. This was especially important in encouraging people to think of what they would like their life to be beyond the hospital environment they were used to. This was also an exciting time for all our nursing staff and they fully supported the changes though by doing so the question of 'what happens to me?' was a natural one for staff when the hostels closed. For those staff they became involved in follow up work with the MAT or elsewhere within the hospital.

In all, I would say, a positive experience for everyone!

It's cool!

By Pete

When asking people recently about how they felt about where they live and their support, one person replied 'it's cool' which, I think, also sums up how I, working in support work, feel as well!

I became interested in working with people when I supported someone to explore their interest in the guitar. Around that time the re-provisioning of the Royal Edinburgh had started and people were beginning to move out of hospital. I enjoyed the work and could see the reward in supporting people to achieve their own goals and ambitions so I applied for a relief worker's post with the organisation I am with now. As they needed to recruit more full time staff I applied as I enjoyed the work and today I work as a service manager. Support work is quite a challenging role but the rewards are huge and you can really see people benefiting.

As quite a lot of people moved out of hospital around the same time it was quite obvious that a lot of planning had been done with individuals in preparation. As a support team we had lots of tools to utilise like Essential Lifestyle Planning (ELP) which really gave us a starting point and background to what people really wanted from life, what they needed and what kind of service we were to provide. It was interesting though to see how this information, created in a hospital environment, became rapidly out of date once people started living in the community. As we got to know people we found that the plans didn't completely reflect the people we were getting to know as another side to them was beginning to surface-people who were making their own choices and in the things that they liked to do.

In the early days of planning people's support we faced a few challenges as it wasn't easy to work out how many hours of support or what types of support people would need until they were faced with the reality of living in their own home. The fine tuning of the support grew out of the knowledge we were gaining of the people we supported. This took a bit of time as we got to know each other and built upon creating trustful and respectful relationships and together we would take the opportunity to just experience the world as it is which can be different to the life of living in a long stay ward. Our teams were created to be flexible and fluid so that we could respond to people saying or evidencing to us that their support was at the wrong time or needing a different kind of support. It was also a time of working out if we, as a staff team, needed more resources or training to make the support work as beneficial as possible. As a team and an organisation it was great seeing what we were part of, aiming towards and seeing the rewards that people were reaping.

At first we did a lot of work to explain what our role was and how the support moulds itself to what people need or want from it. We worked with the MAT team to introduce the concept of a support worker as some people found it strange that we didn't wear badges or uniforms and people would ask us questions about cameras and use of stun guns! We also linked in with people who had already moved out and asked if they would talk to people and show them their homes so that they could get some idea of what to expect and a bit of peer support. We also had to bear in mind that the funding that is there to pay for the support has outcomes that are quite clearly defined by the commissioners as well.

I think for people who had been in hospital for a long time where everything was provided they sometimes struggled with the understanding that it was their house, their shopping list or their gas bill. Basically all the things that go hand in hand with real life which we take for granted and the choices that really we all make in everyday life. Some people got this quite quickly and really flourished whereas others took a bit longer. Sometimes we had to encourage people to realise that they could make a choice of what colour they wanted their home to be, what kind of bed they wanted or what they wanted to eat on Wednesday! To realise that 'yeh, I can choose' and that there is a choice right down to 'yeh, blue is my favourite colour' or 'I do like sugar in my tea' or people asking if it was ok to take a bath in their own bath.

It was really exciting to be part of developing a plan for supporting someone's move into their new house and all the things that they were going to put in it. People would have a grant and we would plan together thinking about balancing what was needed with what someone wanted. We planned because a lot of people didn't have experience of managing their money to get the most out of it and it was really good fun. It could be overwhelming at first with the options that were available and inspiring seeing people make their choices whether in relation to a type of lamp or shade of blue paint.

As people moved into their homes we began supporting people to get to know the locality and introducing them to people within their community. We would use a community mapping process so that we could discover what is in their community. Everyone needs a GP so we would found out where they are and find one that the person would like to register with or where the local shops and bus stops are. We put a lot of effort into supporting people to meet new people and make new connections whether with the library, community centre or pharmacist. It's really about the process of getting to know people and building up relationships so that if someone ever needed to approach someone or ask a question they were going to know them. Some people did feel quite isolated when they first moved out of the hospital and quite cut off from people they had known for years so we also made a lot of effort supporting people to keep in contact with people they had known for ages even though they may now only live round the corner. It was quite a strange thing for some people to pick up a phone and arrange to meet a friend for coffee and a blether. It was also important just to get out and about to enjoy the fun things in life like we all do and it was great spending a few afternoons with someone who loved the dodgems in Portobello.

Whilst in hospital people only had a small amount of money to manage and I think it's fair to say that people managed due to there being a bit of a market system based on barter. When people moved into their own homes and received their full entitlement to benefits some people really understood the financial complexities. For others it was sometimes a bit difficult for them to come to terms with the fact that they had so much money but that they also had the responsibility of paying bills *etc*. With some people having spent a long time in hospital without any real personal secure space they were used to carrying all their valuables around with them. Initially they could be carrying a lot of money about with them which could lead to difficulties. In some of our services systems were created to simplify the responsibility of people managing their own money and some people had to have their money managed for them as part of their care (CTO). We would support people to develop a budgeting plan that they agreed to *e.g.* direct debits to set up payments to the people they had to pay and making sure the money was there so that someone didn't get into difficulties. We also encouraged people to save for bigger things like holidays which a lot of people found difficult. To be honest it's also difficult for me to save for a holiday because if I don't have it deducted at source I spend it!

It's been some time now since the initial resettlement so we have been supporting people for some time and are now working with supporting people who choose to try to take the next step to a more independent life with less support. This is about using person-centred planning and identifying with the person what they need to be responsible for themselves and practising that with their support team. There are lots of ways to do that which encourage growth and independence. For a person who had had problems managing their money in the past we agreed to build up the amount of their own money they managed and take on more responsibility for paying their share of bills *etc.* in a shared house or saving up for a weekend away. By demonstrating that they could manage their money effectively it led to greater independence. Someone else was determined that their Compulsory Treatment Order (CTO) was wrong to manage their money so through discussion with myself and their key worker we decided to challenge the CTO which meant we had to gather lots of evidence to show that this person could manage the £20 a week that they were allowed to draw from Patient Funds-everything else was managed by Patient Funds in the hospital.

Over a period of time we could look back and prove that they had managed their money and had learned a lot from it proving that they weren't going to buy things that they couldn't afford anymore. At a care plan review the person asked to increase the amount and looked to accepting responsibility for other things like a proportion of a house bill so that the person was continually learning how to manage their money but also showing to others that they are developing their ability to do so. Every time they paid for something I would give them a personalised receipt as proof but also to be supportive. The day came when at a review everyone was convinced that the CTO was no longer needed and that person was given back control of managing their own finances which was great. The person has now been on holiday, paid for by themselves, taking their keyworker and had a great time. It felt really good to be part of that, evidencing and challenging some of the judgements that can be made about people.

When I was new to the job I was aware that there was loads to learn in terms of making myself better at my job. I had good support within the team with the training and appraisal system of the organisation really helping. Now, as a manager, I can access training for team members that is relevant to their work and the needs of the people we support. We are always developing as a team so that we can adapt and be flexible as the needs of the people we support change as we all do over time.

In person-centred planning the focus is on dreams and what people want to achieve, what are their goals and ambitions. We all plan in life otherwise how would we be able to pass exams, get on time to an appointment or go on holiday. Breaking down the goal into steps makes it more manageable and you can see your progress. I have heard people really doubt their abilities and describe themselves as 'not having the capacity' yet when working alongside people and supporting them we see people prove to themselves that they can. Did they really believe they 'didn't have capacity' or was that an assessment made of them that they now believed? It is good to celebrate people's achievements and remind people just how far they have come. It's also good to have a record to evidence to others what people have achieved and are capable of. Risk and how services manage risk is an area we can't ignore yet without taking risks how would we develop as people? Which is why good planning really helps the person to think through what they want to do and how they are going to do it safely.

Support work is about helping people to find the best way to do the things they want to do. How would a person who finds crowds difficult but wants to go to a football match achieve their goal? By thinking about all the ways there are to see live football and trying them out. Sunday league games don't attract big crowds but the passion is there and the game is just as competively fought. We all need support to live our lives and make our choices which is how I see support work, by standing alongside someone. It's also about challenging people and where our beliefs come from. I go scuba diving abroad and I can get a bit concerned about how I look in a wetsuit yet once I get there I find a great mix of people and realise that my fears are internal, that I am getting anxious about something I am creating. Understanding this helps me challenge myself and get on with enjoying what I came to do – scuba diving. I am no different from the people I support in that I have my fears and challenges and that I can face them with support, whether from family, friends or professionals.

For many people we support a big challenge for them was being able to prove they were who they said they were! To be able to do so much in life you have to be able to prove who you are yet with many people spending years in hospital they didn't have a fixed address and they had no bills in their name. We supported people to apply for a passport so that this would become their main form of ID. They were then able to do the things most of us take for granted like opening a bank account or applying for a bus pass. People also wanted them so they could start planning holidays abroad.

When we talk of partnership working we don't just mean our partners in Health and Social Care but also within the local community. In supporting people to manage their money independently with less control being placed on them we would build relationships with the local bank. By supporting people with this, the bank staff would get to know the person and if needed an agreement could be put in place to protect people whilst creating the opportunities for people to manage more independently. This was especially important for people who may forget that they have already withdrawn money or where their bank card is. It's about keeping as much control and autonomy as possible with the individual.

As support workers and partners in supporting people, what has been really good is that our Health and Social Care partners have all done what they said they would do and people got the support they needed. Also that we too got the support we needed to do our job. We have supported people to really challenge the values and barriers that can be imposed on them whether by different services or under the Mental Health Act. In encouraging and supporting people to take back control of their life and make their own choices we have made information available and support people in trying and planning new things. It's been wonderful seeing people create their home that reflects themselves and their interests. This is *my* home or where people share, this is *our* house. To see what people have achieved is immensely powerful.

You can be more than you are!

Taking the first step

By Alison Roy

My first experience of supporting people to live in the community was 10 years ago when I started working as a support worker. Our team was working with people who had been long term patients of the REH and who were now moving into their own homes. It was a time of learning new ways for all of us, and we took our time getting to know each other. Sometimes we met with resistance from a few hospital staff who did not believe that some people could manage in the community, predicting a hasty return to hospital.

I set out with the people we were supporting to create homes; offering choices in the colours they wanted to paint rooms, and in the furnishings. At that time, no one felt comfortable in going to the shops, it felt too overwhelming. So choices were made from paint charts and catalogues. When you're already living in the community you take so much for granted and you just get on with being there. Also you don't notice how quickly modern living changed over the last few years; whether it's using cash machines and mobiles or the variety of goods in the supermarket; so I supported people to re-learn their everyday living skills.

Gradually people began to accept that this new place where they lived was actually their home, and most importantly that it was for keeps; or at least for as long as they wanted to be there. As people grew in self confidence, some moved to accommodation where they had more independence. One or two now have their own flat. I feel it has been a privilege to work with people over such a long period, to see how they have grown and changed over the years, trying to make the most of their lives.

Perhaps most telling is that the majority of people have stayed relatively well. If someone becomes ill we can offer extra support. It can make a real difference to a person's recovery if they are able to stay at home where everything is familiar and they remain the focus, rather than the less personal approach of a hospital. I think that this is a tremendous achievement, particularly when some of the people we support had spent a large part of their life in hospital.

It is proof that living in the community does work.

Recovery, reprovisioning, helicopter or tunnel – whatever it takes!

By Carl Abernethy

When I think about my work in mental health services during the last 22 years and when I am speaking to people about recovery, I often think about my contact with those whose experiences and journeys through the mental health system have inspired me. For me, the best way to illustrate this is to use a personal example from my time working with the CRT. When I first met Jenny she was waiting for a place to become available on one of the rehabilitation wards, having been detained in secure and, subsequently, medium secure settings for most of the preceding 20 years. Initially, we talked about her hopes, dreams and aspirations; she described how she wanted to get her own flat, to have the kind of freedom, peace and privacy that was becoming a fading memory from her late teens when she had last lived on her own in the community. She wanted to spend more time with her family and live in her own space where she could listen to and play music.

Although on the surface she was warm, sociable, engaging, and crucially, optimistic; it became clear the more time I spent with her, that the two decades of compulsory detention and the effects of living in psychiatric institutions had eroded much of the hope she had for herself and her future. The planned move to a rehabilitation setting was a step towards life in the community but she had a nagging fear that her stay there would be lengthy and protracted and that she would never leave hospital.

At the time I tried to reassure her that her dream would

come true but I could not predict how long it would take and I feared that the longer she remained in hospital the more disillusioned she would become, making any move, whenever that may have been, more difficult. After several months visiting and spending increasing amounts of time there, Jenny moved to the rehabilitation ward and settled very quickly.

Within a couple of weeks, a remarkable piece of luck presented itself in that a place in a shared flat became available in one of the support services funded and managed through re-provisioning. What could be considered another significant piece of luck or coincidence was that Jenny knew the existing occupant and prospective flat-mate (having spent time in hospital with her some years before). They had been friends but had not had contact for many years. Within minutes of us all meeting at the flat it was clear that this could really work. Four weeks later Jenny moved into the flat.

Jenny made a remarkable transition to life in the community. Her personality shone through and she quickly developed relationships with support staff whose person-centred, welcoming and open approach made Jenny feel at home. They helped with practical things like sorting out benefits, registering with a GP, organising routines for medication, appointments, budgeting, shopping, cooking and housework, and helped her decorate and furnish her room the way she wanted it. She was able, for the first time in many years, to spend time with her family when she wanted, attending birthday parties for her brothers and sisters, nieces and nephews and going on family holidays. It was an environment she flourished in and she experienced no major setbacks or re-admissions to hospital.

Two years later I moved to a post with the MHO team but remained in contact with Jenny, her support network and family. Jenny was on a (community-based) CTO so when the opportunity arose for me to become Jenny's allocated mental health officer we all agreed this made sense as we had an established relationship. Subsequently, when her CTO was due for extension, in discussion with Jenny, her mother, support staff and her Psychiatrist, we agreed that it was no longer necessary and it was allowed to lapse. I think this was a fantastic achievement for her as it was the first time in well over 20 years that she was not subject to any form of compulsory measures under mental health legislation. This acknowledged how far she had come and how able she was to take control of aspects of her life previously denied to her.

It is now almost five years since Jenny left hospital and she has still not spent another night there. She is happy, fulfilled and content, gets on well with her flatmate and never misses a family gathering or holiday. She has considerably less contact with her support staff but knows that they are only a phone call away if she needs them. She doesn't look back.

Some may think that Jenny has been blessed with a good measure of good fortune. This story's linear nature and lack of major setbacks and its happy ending may make it sound unbelievable, but it happened and Jenny is living the life she wants to lead. The relationship we had, the relationships she has with other people and the fact that everything fell into place, all makes me believe that this can and should happen for everyone. But this wouldn't have happened if the infra-structure and resources had not been in place to allow it to happen, or without the belief and high expectations of the teams and individuals involved. Hundreds of people have benefited from similar processes and continue to do so, many with the continuing support of those involved but thousands more people remain trapped in hospitals for decades or tied up in cycles of admission-discharge-readmission for decades, prevented from regaining control over, or living their lives. Jenny has regained control of her life and how she leads it because those around her provided the environment for her to take back that control. Jenny's story and my involvement at this crucial time gives inspiration to me and reinforces my belief that recovery can and does happen and that with the environments we create, what we do and the relationships we have with people, do make a difference.

I have often thought that 'hope,' although considered central, and a key element in recovery, by its usual definition, leaves too much to chance, and that not enough importance is given to the issue of control. But now, for me, the following quote bridges that gap and defines it as a fuel for perseverance and taking responsibility for carrying on the struggle.

'Hope is not blind optimism. It's not ignoring the enormity of the task ahead, or the roadblocks that stand in our path. It's not sitting on the sidelines or shirking from a fight. Hope is that thing inside us that insists, despite all the evidence to the contrary, that something better awaits us if we have the courage to reach for it, work for it, and fight for it.' Barack Obama

And finally...!

Alison Robertson and Lesley Smith

On behalf of the Patients' Council as we bring 'Stories of Changing Lives,' to a conclusion, we would like to share with you some reflections from ourselves.

We can confidently say that by having people who believe in us, recognising our strengths and potential, seeing each of us as an individual with a history and believe that the future doesn't have to be limited to a diagnosis, change becomes a reality. Real possibility is within our hands when we are encouraged to take control, follow our interests, have dreams and aspirations and, like anyone else, take risks! Relationships are central as we realise that first and foremost they are what supports our growth and change as 'no man is an island.'

It's inspirational to read how people have developed their lives and risen to their challenges. Supporting people with the person-centred philosophy and practice which was at the heart of the whole re-provisioning process was vital. It highlights the differences to people's quality of life when paid support is individualised rather than a person fitting into a system. People are more than psychiatric patients, not just defined by a diagnosis and symptoms but with skills, preferences, relationships and goals.

What maybe stands out from this project is that it highlights a system that was there for patients to fit into, and hence not always as effective, rather than a service that helps all individuals on their own path to recovery – 'living as independently as possible with or without symptoms.' This person-centred approach, evidenced here through people's experiences, has shown itself to be something that really works within service provision. The Patients' Council applauds and supports good practice that improves the experiences of people while they are patients and support when living at home. We think that when mental health services adopt this approach as the prevailing culture and philosophy then people can recover their lives. For some people that would mean they wouldn't find themselves in a cycle of repeatedly returning to hospital and staff would have a greater sense of job satisfaction as they see people moving on with their support and help. As a result, everyone benefits!

Reflecting on peoples experiences, as told here, really makes us aware of the crucial importance of defining the words 'care' and 'support', and how they are delivered in services. There is a disabling kind of care and an empowering type of support. This reminds us of the old adage 'that it is better to give a starving man a rod and teach him to fish, that he may feed himself, rather than keep giving him a fish each day'. The former gives control back to the individual. The support offered to people involved in moving out of the REH has been an empowering one of encouragement thus enabling people to take back control of their own lives. Control is something which can easily be lost when admitted to hospital but especially when you have lived there for a long period of time. It's vital to remember and question the power of the institution and ensure that people, when patients, have as much control as possible and for services to work in partnership with them. The other kind of help that only maintains people and suppresses symptoms is ultimately disabling and can lead to a stalemate. To live a fulfilled life people need more than a focus on medication stabilisation! By shifting the focus to living to one's full potential whilst managing the challenges to one's mental health is vital. A person with angina may not be able to run a marathon but can live a meaningful life in many other regards. Different illness, same principle.

Finally, may we say how moved we were by the experiences shared with us by all our contributors. To read their experiences can help others understand that peoples' lives don't have to be limited because they have spent time in hospital and that they can have support that meets their needs and enables them to live the life they choose. From the reflections and contributions of those who support people we realise and appreciate that the wellbeing and future of each individual is their focus. They give us a sense of how much they believe in people and their potential along with their commitment and passion to supporting people by 'working with' rather than 'doing to or for'.

We would like to thank everyone on behalf of the Patients' Council for sharing their experiences in this publication and wish everyone all the very best for their future.

Thankyou.

'Recovery is being able to live a meaningful and satisfying life, as defined by each person, in the presence or absence of symptoms. It is about having control over and input into your own life. Each individual's recovery, like his or her experience of the mental health problems or illness, is a unique and deeply personal process. It is important to be clear that there is no right or wrong way to recover.'

SRN 'Journeys of Recovery'

Glossary

Acute ward Admission ward for adults. Edinburgh is divided into sectors with GP practices determining which ward a person would be admitted to.

CTO Compulsory Treatment Order (Community Based) – Mental Health Law which allows the compulsory treatment of individuals with mental disorder who live in the community.

CRT Community Rehabilitation Team – a smaller team that replaced MAT to continue the resettlement of people into the community and provide on-going care management.

DLA Disability Living Allowance, a non means tested State benefit paid to people with a disability and/or support needs. There are two components that can be awarded – Care and Mobility.

Edinburgh Mental Health Partnership Representative group of service users, carers, service providers, NHS and local authority staff overseeing the re-provisioning of hospital based care within the community.

Incapax A system where people are required to have their money managed for them.

Hostel The REH had a number of hostels in the Morningside area housing 49 people.

MAT Multi-Agency Team of ten care managers from professional backgrounds in Health, Social Work and the voluntary sector combining roles to create a more user-friendly, integrated and accessible service. The team offered each of the 170 people living in the hostels or four continuing care wards planning for their future using person-centred planning. This led to 92 people being discharged to the newly commissioned community tenancies and support. Funding ceased in 2002 with around 70 people moving into re-provisioning tenancies and another 20 preparing to move later that year. A few others also moved into other community tenancies or with other social care providers.

Mental Health (Care and Treatment) (Scotland) Act 2003 Mental Health Law in relation to people assessed as having a mental disorder and their carers.

MHO A Mental Health Officer is a specially trained social worker who deals with people with mental disorder and has particular duties under the Act.

Mental Health Tribunal The Mental Health Tribunal for Scotland was set up by the Act to make decisions about the compulsory care and treatment of people with mental disorder.

North Wing Rehabilitation ward within the REH.

Realising Recovery Training in values based practice provided by Lothain Recovery Network and open to people who use services, their carers and workers. Workbook developed between NHS Education Scotland (NES) and Scottish Recovery Network (SRN).

REH Royal Edinburgh Hospital A psychiatric hospital providing services including acute, rehabilitation and continuing care for people who experience difficulties with their mental health.

Re-provisioning In this case the Edinburgh Joint Mental Health Plan in 1997 looked to cut 92 continuing care beds in the REH from a total of 170. Bridging finance enabled the creation of 92 community placements for people as an alternative to hospital.

SRN Scottish Recovery Network – national organisation for all promoting the reality of recovery. www.scottishrecovery.net

Support Organisation/Provider Social Care Providers who support people to live in their own homes and live life as they choose. Re-provisioning involved commissioning Social Care providers to support people in a mix of community based tenancies. Organisations providing support to people in this re-provisioning process were Barony, Carr-Gomm Scotland, Link Living, Places for People (formerly known as Edinvar), Richmond Fellowship and SAMH. Other social care providers provided support in their established services on an individual basis.

Glossary 89

Stories of changing lives